Best Things in Life

236 Favorite Things About
CLEVELAND

(*by Clevelanders*)

Edited by Christopher Johnston

GRAY & COMPANY, PUBLISHERS • CLEVELAND

GRAY & COMPANY, PUBLISHERS
11000 Cedar Avenue
Cleveland, Ohio 44106
(216) 721-2665

ISBN 0-9631738-8-X

Printed in the United States of America

SECOND PRINTING

INTRODUCTION

Except for a few college years spent in upstate New York, I have lived my life in Cleveland. For decades, then, I have heard it said that the best things in life are all right here.

At first this saying was a defensive posture taken by citizens of a beleaguered city experiencing a string of public relations nightmares–most of which had to do with either bodies of water or bodies of mayors. More recently, it has become the proud boast of a remarkable urban renaissance.

But to my knowledge, for all they are touted, no one has ever collected the Best Things in one place. That's what this book sets out to do.

To find out what's best about Cleveland, I decided to go to the only authoritative source: Clevelanders themselves. I distributed postcards throughout the city and suburbs at various public locations urging Clevelanders to "Have Your Say." I also contacted a number of notable Clevelanders, some current and some who have moved to careers elsewhere. Finally, I buttonholed family and friends and even conducted a few on-the-street interviews.

Aside from an occasional dose of cynicism, the responses were very thoughtful, very thorough. The variety was impressive, and there were many surprises (including a common obsession with orange barrels). The process was also an eye-opener. There was the time my call was screened by a prominent CEO's secretary's secretary. That's power!

One of the biggest challenges was waking up every day and realizing there were a dozen more people I should contact. Of course, every time I mentioned the project to people they would suggest five others. I couldn't reach everyone—all the more reason for a second volume!

I found after starting the project just how difficult it is for Cleveophiles like myself to pin down two or three favorite aspects of the city. As for my choice, I would have to say the Garden Court and the sculpture courtyard at the Cleveland Museum of Art are two of the most restorative spaces I have ever experienced in the world.

Difficult as choosing a favorite is, Clevelanders presented me with hundreds. The 236 included here were selected based on originality, aptness, style, and whim. (There were duplicate responses, so sometimes I had to choose one to represent many. I apologize to those who may recognize their response under someone else's name; the other guy just got there first.)

Some of the responses were shortened slightly to fit the format, but I tried not to tamper much with anyone's wording. The list is in no particular order, though there are a few intended juxtapositions. I must confess that I also did not try to verify any best-in-the-world claims. Hey, who am I to question?

The list won't be complete, of course, until you send in your response. Until then I'm confident it can be declared the definitive list, according to Clevelanders, of the absolute best things in life. Enjoy them.

—Christopher Johnston

ACKNOWLEDGEMENTS

In addition to all who took the time to respond, I would like to thank Margaret Rose and the sixth grade class at Emerson Middle School in Lakewood for their enthusiastic contributions, Lenore "Tribemeister" Stoakes for her help in tracking Indians, and Patrice for shouldering much of the survey distribution and providing her usual assiduous support.

1. Cleveland is down home, international,
    and people-friendly.
    —*Michael R. White, Mayor*

2. My favorite things about Cleveland are the public-private partnerships and "together, we can do it" spirit which were and still are responsible for Cleveland's ongoing renaissance.

   —*George V. Voinovich, Governor*

3. Autumn: apples, pumpkins, the smell of the leaves, the Browns at the stadium—There's nothing like Cleveland in the fall, not anywhere. And I've been around.

   —*Greg Harbaugh, NASA Space Shuttle Astronaut*

4. A rush hour that only locals would notice.

   —*Dr. Richard Ehrlich, Executive Director, Western Reserve Historical Society*

5. Cleveland does Vivaldi's music proud: We have an authentic autumn, a wondrous winter, a sprightly spring and a sumptuous summer.

   —*Karen Gabay, Principal Dancer, Cleveland Ballet*

6. The exciting variety of whatever-nationality-you're-in-the-mood-for restaurants.

   —*Maria I., Cleveland*

Houses we can afford on streets where we want to live, with plenty of shady trees, green grass, and good neighbors.

8. A feeling of optimism that makes you proud to be a member of the community.
   —*Wilma Smith, Anchor, WJW TV-8*

9. High school football teams. St. Ignatius in particular.
   —*Phoenix J., Cleveland*

10. It's a wonderful place to raise a family, as my wife and I have done for 30+ years.

    —*Dr. Robert White, Director of Neurosurgery, MetroHealth Medical Center*

11. Being pretentious is a complete waste of time here.

    —*Thomas O., Cleveland*

12. Neighborhood bars. You don't find them in newer cities.

    —*Dan Coughlin, Sportscaster, WJW TV-8*

13. Cleveland has the best workplace in the United States: Jacobs Field.

    —*Mike Hargrove, Manager, Cleveland Indians*

14. Duck hunting in the marshes off Lake Erie.
   —*Mal Mixon, President, Chairman & CEO,*
   Invacare Corporation

15. The Festival of Lights on the river is the best.
   —*Cheryl G., Lakewood*

16. The people: Some of the friendliest people in the country, except to visiting teams when they play the Browns.

    —*Don Shula, Head Coach, Miami Dolphins*

17. I love looking at the boats and the water while I'm driving home on the Shoreway.

    —*Denise Dufala, Anchor/Reporter,*
    WOIO TV-19

18. Sports. From every major league sport that has a team here to softball with young boys and girls and old men all playing the same game . . . from exciting high school football to playing football in the city streets . . . from bowling to bocci ball.

—*Big Chuck Schodowski, "Big Chuck & Lil' John Show," WJW TV-8*

19. Malley's hot fudge sundaes. With peanuts. Two cherries.

   —*Diane J., Brecksville*

20. Forget San Francisco. If you want to see bridges, go to Cleveland.

   —*Ian B., Lakewood*

21. Listening to the world-renowned Cleveland Orchestra, both at Severance and Blossom.

   —*Dr. Robert P. Bergman, Director,*
   Cleveland Museum of Art

22. Bay Village's Huntington Beach at dusk in August. The view is phenomenal!

   —*Liz Claman, Morning Exchange Anchor,*
   WEWS TV-5

23. When I got here in 1986, the people were just extremely friendly and helped take my family in. Our friends have grown as my family has grown here.

—*Mark Price, Point Guard, Cleveland Cavaliers*

24. I like to pet the animals at Lake Farmpark.

—*Ashley R., Willoughby Hills*

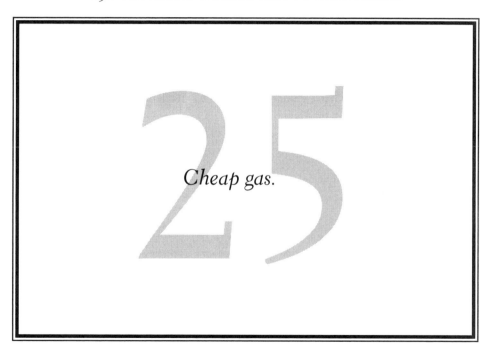

Cheap gas.

26. The ethnic, cultural, social and economic diversity of the city.

   —*Harvey Pekar, Cartoonist, Creator of American Splendor Comics*

27. Biological diversity: We're at the intersection of three physiographic regions.

   —*David Beach, Environmentalist/Writer*

28. Saturday morning hockey at the Cleveland Skating Club.

   —*George Gund III, San Francisco, Elko, Cleveland*

29. I like the public libraries. I go to the library almost every week.

   —*Henry M., Euclid*

30. You can go from Cedar Point to the Rain Forest to the Rock and Roll Hall of Fame to the new stadium and arena to Geauga Lake to Sea world to the Football Hall of Fame back to Akron to the Inventors Hall of Fame. There's plenty to do.

— *Jerry Gordon, Publisher, Sun Newspapers*

31. Cleveland is outside The Beltway.

    —*George Stephanopoulos, Senior Advisor to the President, The White House*

32. The Regional Transportation System: It's always been there for me through my many working years and for enjoying varied recreations. Surely our bus drivers are among Cleveland's best PR people.

    —*Maxine L., Cleveland*

33. For us horse enthusiasts, South and North Chagrin Metropark Reservations have excellent bridle trails—a rarity in modern suburbs.

   —*Lizbeth K., Chagrin Falls*

34. People watching!

   —*Mary B., Hudson*

35. Hearing the seafood vendor yell "Neeext!" to wait on you at a West Side Market fish stand.

   —*Rich and Janet J., Cleveland Heights*

36. We're only 1-1/4 hours from the dirt roads of Wayne County's Amish country.

   —*Brenda Lewison, Editor, Northeast Ohio Avenues*

37. My only complaint is I had too happy a childhood in Cleveland. It didn't prepare me for what the rest of life was going to be like.

    —*Ian Frazier, Author/Writer*

38. Watching the parades from my dad's office in the BP Building.

    —*Christy B., Lakewood*

39. It's a 3-D city: Diverse, dynamic, and delightful.

    —*Ned Y., Cleveland Heights*

40. The downtown skyline from the Red Line Rapid Transit as you approach the W. 117 Street station.

    —*David B., Lakewood*

41. Ethnic picnics: There's nothing like working a crowd to the beat of polka music.
    —*Dennis Kucinich, Politician, Former Mayor of Cleveland*

42. My Cleveland Heights neighborhood.
    —*Roger Danforth, Interim Artistic Director, The Cleveland Play House*

43. I can live in a suburb 6.5 miles from my office downtown, which you can't do in many cities. I like the fact that you can drive here. In some cities you can't have a car.

     —*Jane Scott, World's Oldest Rock Reporter, The Plain Dealer*

44. A vibrant original music scene.

     —*Mark Holan, Editor, Scene Magazine*

45. Seeing downtown lighted for a Monday Night Football Game.

   —*Art Modell, Owner and President,*
   Cleveland Browns

46. Living the American Dream in a fun, up-and-coming city.

   —*Perry Ganchar, Right Wing,*
   Cleveland Lumberjacks

47. The joy of victory after making it to the top of Cedar Hill during an ice storm.

48. The roller-coaster thrill of driving down Cedar Hill during an ice storm.

    —*Sandy Siebenschuh, Editor-in-Chief, Cleveland Enterprise*

49. Housing is an incredible bargain here, especially if you've spent any time on either coast. A cottage there equals a castle here.

    —*Nick B., Willoughby*

50. America's most abundant and fertile farm ponds, where I can test myself behind an ultra-light rod and line or catch supper whenever I choose.

    —*Ted Henry, Anchor, WEWS TV-5*

*Serious barbecued ribs. And people
who know how to enjoy them.*

52. Most of us have difficult soil and erratic weather but great gardens. That says something about our Cleveland character.

    —*Susan McClure, Writer*

53. The pastas and pizzas—in all of their authentic, garlicky glory—available in Little Italy.

    —*Lori V., Chardon*

54. The Children's Museum on Saturday offers great drama as single mothers who are members try to pick up single fathers who are members. It's better than the soaps.

    —*Ted Schwarz, Author*

55. The Children's Museum is an intellectual playground disguised as a really fun place.

    —*Meredith M., Lakewood*

56. This city gives you as much as you're willing to put into it.

    —*Jack Kahl, Jr., Chairman and CEO,
    Manco, Inc.*

57. An art museum, a contemporary art center, and an alternative art center all free to the public.

    —*Cathryn Kapp, President & Creative Director,
    Kapp & Associates*

58. Getting around, getting to where I want is pretty easy. The more I see other cities, the more I appreciate how easy it is to get around.

    —*Thomas Bier, Director of Housing Research Program, Cleveland State University*

59. It is 350 miles from my in-laws. It is 350 miles from my family.

    —*Jim C., Lakewood*

60. I enjoyed being the first black player in the American League representing Cleveland. It's a fine city, and I have come back many times. The people are good people, nice people, and the fans are great fans.

    —*Larry Doby, Retired Baseball Player, Cleveland Indians*

61. The Indians: They've always been different from the rest of major league baseball, whether we're winning 111 out of 154 and losing four straight in the World Series or clinching the first Wild Card playoff slot in a season ended by a strike.

   —*Lenore S., Mentor*

62. Watching the Blue Angels perform 100 feet off the ground at Burke Lakefront Airport on Labor Day.

   Mukul M., Westlake

63. Playhouse Square: See all the best shows right in your home town.

   —Phoenix J., Cleveland

64. Pork. Cleveland butchers do great pork: Zagrab's smoked bacon and meaty ham hocks, Ye Olde Sausage Shoppe kielbasi, West Side Market chorizo.

    —*Michael Ruhlman, Senior Editor, Northern Ohio LIVE*

65. The Health Museum.

    —*Natalie C., Cleveland*

66. Antique row on Lorain Avenue on the near West Side. Anything from a slant-sided, spring-hinged two-door, non-automatic toaster (c. 1930s), to a porcelain-and-brass finial just like the one that's missing from dear Aunt Aggie's table lamp.

    —*Patricia H., Mentor On The Lake*

67. Karamu House.

    —*Joyce A., Cleveland*

Warm sand and cool breezes, kite-flying and beach reading at Edgewater, Huntington, or Mentor Headlands.

69. I've traveled all over the U.S., and nowhere are the people more friendly, caring and helpful. You can ask for the time of day, and suddenly ten people within earshot are looking at their watches. Folks who move away usually end up coming back to stay.

—*Tom H., Cleveland*

70. Whenever it gets over 90 degrees on the West Side, the old timers open up the garage door, get out a lawn chair, and sit around drinking beer in the shade.

   —*Bert Z., Broadview Heights*

71. The operative word when talking about Cleveland is "vivid." We have vivid seasons, a vivid cultural scene, and vivid people who live real lives.

   —*Ernie Krivda, Jazz Musician*

72. People are friendly, lots of family-oriented communities.

   —*Carlos Baerga, Second Basemen,*
   Cleveland Indians

73. Only in Cleveland would people actually wait in line to get into the "Dawg Pound."

   —*R. Douglas Cowan, President & CEO,*
   The Davey Tree Expert Company

74. The religious community takes an active role in community leadership, innovative human service initiatives, and helps alleviate human suffering at all levels of society.

    —*Rev. Kenneth Chalker, 1st United Methodist Church, Cleveland*

75. The Cleveland Restoration Society.

    —*Thomas Pervanje, Pervanje/Henderson Architects, Twinsburg*

76. Suburban living, with easy access to University Circle and downtown cultural riches.

    —*Patience and Harry C., Cleveland Heights*

77. The lake is an incredible asset; it gives me renewed strength daily.

    —*Denise Fugo, President & Co-Owner, Sammy's*

78. They didn't film my favorite Christmas movie in Cleveland for nothing (A Christmas Story)! From snow-covered Shaker Square, where I welcomed Santa back in the '40s and later took my children, to Chagrin Falls; from historic Bedford Commons to Tower City and Public Square; there's nowhere in America that better exemplifies the spirit of the holidays than Cleveland.

—*Tim Taylor, Anchor, WJW TV-8*

79. The thrills of the Cleveland Grand Prix in July! The hottest event of the summer on the North Coast.

   —*Lee Jordan, Live on Five, WEWS TV-5*

80. The magnificent water dance at Tower City can't be seen anywhere else.

   —*Abby L., Lakewood*

81. History: Without Cleveland, U.S. history would have huge, empty gaps. The list is long, but any town with the bodies of John D. Rockefeller and Balto, the dog who inspired the Iditarod, just has to be one hell of a town.

    —*John H. Tidyman, Writer*

82. Looking out over the Jacobs Field scoreboard on a hot July night, seeing the Cleveland skyline.

   —Clayton Deutsch, Managing Director, McKinsey & Company

83. Cleveland Orchestra on Thursday nights— a who's who of the city and sublime music.

   —Ned Whelan, Whelan Communications

More than 130 bookstores ought to satisfy any booklover.

85. My old neighborhood at W. 127 and Lorain is still intact, and I can visit to relive old memories anytime I want.

   —*Joseph Roman, Executive Director, Cleveland Tomorrow*

86. During holidays I like driving around and looking at everybody's decorations.

   —*Alexandra T., Lakewood*

87. Cleveland has the best college radio scene in the U.S. Incredibly eclectic and always interesting. At any given time, one station might be playing Tibetan chants, another will have a live performance by some guy playing a saw, and another one will be doing a 24-hour tribute to the Sex Pistols.

—*Thomas Owens, Shanghai Club*

88. Where else could I share my favorite jewelry with the whole city? It's the beautiful "Emerald Necklace!" Cleveland's Metroparks.

   —*Mary Poldruhi, Proprietor, Parma Pierogies Restaurants*

89. Rock and Roll Hall of Fame: Rock 'n Roll is here to stay, here in Cleveland!!

   —*Carl Walz, NASA Space Shuttle Astronaut*

90. Brothership between black and white.
   —*Esam A., Cleveland*

91. The wonderful mix of people gives
   Cleveland its basic Midwestern values,
   which are quite different from many other
   places in the U.S.
   —*Bob Gries, President, Gries Investments*

92. The Lake is a mesmerizing and beautiful body of water. To live in a city on water has always seemed to me an extra privilege.

    —*Hal Holbrook, Actor*

93. Night after night of spectacular sunsets over Lake Erie from our West Side vantage point.

    —*Ron & Alice W., Rocky River*

94. All the green (grass, Metroparks, Cuyahoga Valley National Recreational Area): Take a trip to LA or New York, then see how the color embraces you upon your return.

    —*John Urbancich, Executive Editor, Sun Newspapers*

95. Southeast Harley-Davidson.

    —*Clyde Z., Chesterland*

96. Waking up to six inches of partly cloudy in the winter.

    —*John L., Strongsville*

97. Buying pumpkins and Christmas trees at the Miles Farmers Market.

    —*Lucinda T., Pepper Pike*

98. A spectacular legacy of magnificent trees, one of the reasons I chose to live in Cleveland Heights.

    —*Brenda Lewison, Editor, Northeast Ohio Avenues*

99. Lots of historic architecture, Victorian homes, churches, and the renaissance of areas like Tremont and Ohio City.

    —*Magnolia N., Cleveland*

100. We have exceptionally fine statuary, excellent bronze works around the Cleveland Museum of Art and University Circle area, the Soldiers and Sailors Monument, etc.

—*Greg J., Mayfield Heights*

101. Hellacious, window-rattling, sleep-depriving, child-scream-inducing, Zeus-worthy, middle-of-the-night thunderstorms.

—*June O., Medina*

102

Any time the Browns, Indians, Cavs, Crunch, Lumberjacks, or Thunderbolts win.

103. Best five months of golf anywhere. Many lovely, accessible, and affordable courses, great grass, much sunshine, made even better by the worst seven months of anything, anywhere.

    —*Rich G., Shaker Heights*

104. The friendly people who live here and their Midwestern values.

    —*James B., Moreland Hills*

105. Cleveland has enough muck to rake to last me two to three lifetimes.

    —*Roldo Bartimole, Writer*

106. The Gateway Complex is a dream come true.

    —*Lori V., Parma*

107. Walking through Lake View Cemetery on a fall day—taking a peek in to Wade Chapel (designed by Tiffany himself).

    —*Liz Ludlow, Editor, Cleveland Magazine*

108. Woof, woof, woof!

    —*A. Fan, Dawg Pound*

109. The best place to meet that "special some-one." I ought to know. I met my wife here, and I'm from Seattle, WA.

    Gary H., Cleveland

110. Honey Hut Ice Cream.

    —Carlo Wolff, Writer

111. People who visit may know about the nationally recognized symbols, such as the Terminal Tower or the Indians, but we also have a broad range of great educational facilities, from the universities to the prestigious prep schools and high schools to our teaching hospitals.

—*Barry R., Gates Mills*

112

The best backyards in America for playing kick-the-can, jumping through sprinklers, or just going barefoot.

113. The roar of Lake Erie cresting against the cliffs during a winter storm. The power of the winds and waves holds me to nature even while I'm in the city.

      —*Anne Gordon, Editor, Sunday, The Plain Dealer*

114. A starry sky and the Cleveland Orchestra on the lawn at Blossom Music Center.

      —*Janet M., University Heights*

115. The best corned beef delis in the world.
      —*Michael C., Shaker Heights*

116. All the wonderful, professionally minded
      and talented actors, designers, and theater
      artists who make Cleveland their home.
      —*Lucia Colombi, Artistic Director,*
      Ensemble Theatre

117. The people: The way they love and support one of their own. Their love of city traditions and their great attitude. Cleveland is the biggest "small town" in the world.

    —*Big Chuck Schodowski, "Big Chuck & Lil' John Show," WJW TV-8*

118. Spring: All the yards are yellow in beauty, the dandelions are in bloom!

    —*Annette R., Brook Park*

119. City neighborhoods: Cleveland's cultural diversity makes it possible to visit many different "countries" in a single day.

    —*Dennis Kucinich, Politician, Former Mayor of Cleveland*

120. The scale of the urban area offers big city advantages without being overwhelming.

    —*David Beach, Environmentalist/Writer*

121. Watching the ore boats ply up and down the river (especially at Collision Bend) from a riverside restaurant in the Flats.

     —*George Gund III, San Francisco, Elko, Cleveland*

122. Summer, not winter.

     —*Robert B., Cleveland Heights*

123. Downtown for shopping—variety.
     —*Marilyn V., Concord*

124. Looking forward to a new season for the
     Cavs at the Gund Arena.
     —*Dr. Robert P. Bergman, Director,*
     Cleveland Museum of Art

125. The banana and cranberry juice protein shake at the River Oaks Racquet Club in Rocky River—Mike makes it up special!

   —*Liz Claman, Morning Exchange Anchor, WEWS TV-5*

126. Fourth-of-July fireworks for all, on the sand at Edgewater.

   —*Eric R., Beachwood*

Public sculpture everywhere: beautiful and surprising, elegant and shocking. From the venerable Hope Memorial Bridge pylons to the controversial Free Stamp.

128. Any diner on lower St. Clair or Superior. Cheapest and best breakfast in the U.S.A. Shay's, Fifth Wheel, Slyman's . . . They're all great.

     —*Robert Griffin, President, Scat Records*

129. A Nautica Queen cruise is a steak on the lake.

     —*Eric R., Parma*

130. Distances in Cleveland are manageable. Drive west from the Heights area for twenty minutes and you're in the excitement of downtown. Drive east for 20 minutes and you're in the pastoral rolling horse country of Geauga and Lake Counties.

   —*Robert Conrad, President and Broadcast Manager, WCLV FM-95.5*

131. The East Cleveland Public Library: Free
jazz concerts, free professional writing
training, free Wednesday night science/
math program for kids and families, free
computer training and use, not to mention
books. And all based in a low-income area.

—*Ted Schwarz, Author*

132. Relative to other places, good living standards at low cost.
    —*Gary G., Shaker Heights*

133. Wilbert's Bar & Grille: Best live music club in the country, obscure acts up close.
    —*Michael Heaton, Minister of Culture,*
    The Plain Dealer

134. Bird-watching at Shaker Lakes.
   —*Michelle C., Rocky River*

135. The Indians and Jacobs Field: You gotta be
   tough to keep waiting 'till next year.
   —*Jeff Maynor, Anchor, WKYC TV-3*

136. Home of the sportingest walleye on the planet. (And tasty perch.)
   —*Jim S., Strongsville*

137. Christmas Lights at Nela Park.
   —*Jim N., Lyndhurst*

138. When I was growing up, rather than go to my local branch, I used to take a bus downtown to the Cleveland Public Library. I loved to read. The marble staircases were great. So many books, and it was all for free!

    —*Drew Carey, Comedian*

139. Leadership.

    —*Barbara Bisset, President, Bisset Steel*

140. Driving east to Middlefield in the fall to check out the foliage, pick up some Amish cheese and ham, and maybe dine at the Middlefield Tavern.

    —*Stephanie P., Solon*

141. New York Spaghetti House.

    —*Mike D., Lakewood*

142. Cleveland's trying to improve itself. The downtown area is improving. The Flats have been developed. You've got a hall of fame there now. You have a new stadium for baseball. You still have the Browns!

—*Jim Brown, NFL Football Hall of Famer, Cleveland Browns*

This may be the best place in the world to get sick. (Because, with The Cleveland Clinic, University Hospitals, MetroHealth, and others, it is the best place to get well!)

144. Walking around Edgewater Park, watching the water ski macho dudes wipeout.

    —*Mike Shea, Publisher, Alternative Press*

145. We have the most overbuilt highway system in the country. It was designed for 3.5 million people; we have 1.2 million.

    —*Jerry Gordon, Publisher, Sun Newspapers*

146. The Metropark Zoo's Rainforest brings the tropics to Cleveland.
    —*Derek W., Shaker Heights*

147. Chiles Rellenos at LaFiesta Restaurant.
    —*Mal Mixon, President, Chairman & CEO, Invacare Corporation*

148. Yellow traffic lights turning red mean "speed up and go." Yellow means it's not over yet.

    —*Dr. Jerry Sue Thornton, President, Cuyahoga Community College, Metro Campus*

149. St. Patrick's Church (Bridge Avenue) is evidence of the influence of Irish Culture.

    —*Joan M., Cleveland*

150. One of the things I liked when I moved here from Utah was the strong sense of history that we don't have in the West. Yet people here are not afraid to build on the bones of their grandparents and use the past as fertilizer for growth in the future.

    —*Morgan Lund, Actor*

151. Even short people have a chance to grow in this town.

    —*Michael R. White, Mayor*

152. Fall walks in the Metroparks.
    —*Bob Stevens, Sportscaster, WEWS TV-5*

153. My friends from out of town are always
    overwhelmed by the wealth of activities
    here. On any night, you can go out and
    find plenty to do.
    —*Allison K., Olmsted Falls*

154. The public education system in Shaker Heights.

    —*Gary Sangster, Executive Director,*
    Cleveland Center for Contemporary Art

155. West Side Market: Best selection and best prices on freshest food in town. Plus the people-watching alone is worth a trip.

    —*Denise J., Cleveland*

156. It's easy to tell the change of seasons:
Orange barrels up: spring, summer, fall.
Orange barrels down: winter.
—*Katherine Boyd, Reporter, WEWS TV-5*

157. Cleveland Stadium has the best hot dogs.
—*Magda M., Lakewood*

158. The renovation of the Cleveland neighbor-
     hoods.

     —*Laronda M., Cleveland*

159. The beauty and architectural diversity of
     the great homes in the Heights, offset by
     ancient trees, gardens of shrubs and flowers
     through all the seasons.

     —*Gerald Freedman, Artistic Director,
     Great Lakes Theater Festival*

160. Professionally, it's a wonderful place to
work. A very compatible, comfortable, very
exciting place.

— *Dr. Robert White, Director of Neurosurgery,*
MetroHealth Medical Center

161. Ribs at the Tick-Tock Tavern.

— *George Stephanopoulos, Senior Advisor to*
the President, The White House

162. The Arcade just before closing.
     —*Bill Gunlocke, Publisher*

163. Riding the slow, dark service elevator, with
     gate and operator, up to the Smart Bar in
     the Flats.
     —*Rich and Janet J., Cleveland Heights*

164. The way lake perch ride the crest of an
      enormous white cap and land on the East
      Shoreway during rush hour.
      —*David B., Lakewood*

165. Predictable weather! It's always unpre-
      dictable!
      —*Ted Stepien, President, Classified USA*

166

Dinner in an old warehouse, drinks in an old powerhouse, and dancing by the riverside after work on Friday.

167. No one makes a polish boy the way we do in Cleveland.

   —*Paula F., Cleveland*

168. World-class pierogies—on both sides of town—prepared so many wonderful, different ways!

   —*Rena Blumberg, Public Relations Director, WDOK/WRMR*

169. Staying home: There are great houses in Cleveland, and I like to use them.
  —*Michael Ruhlman, Senior Editor,*
  Northern Ohio LIVE

170. You can get to the airport from almost anywhere in town in 20-30 minutes.
  —*Michael D., Chagrin Falls*

171. World Series time, no traffic jams downtown.
    —*Paul B., Parma*

172. The West Side Market is truly unique. I can't imagine planning an important meal without it.
    —*Roger Danforth, Interim Artistic Director, The Cleveland Play House*

173. Cleveland was a great place to grow up
      because there was an awful lot of culture
      and excitement, but not so much that you
      didn't have to make things up on your own.
      That's why there are a lot of comedians and
      humor writers from Cleveland. It has a very
      good ratio of excitement and boredom, very
      healthy for your development.

      —*Ian Frazier, Author/Writer*

174. Chagrin Falls because it is this gem of nature that has been allowed to retain its charm and wildness in the midst of a quintessential American Main Street.
— *Gerald Freedman, Artistic Director, Great Lakes Theater Festival*

175. The thing I like is the friendliness of the people.
— *Hal Lebovitz, Sports Writer Emeritus, The Plain Dealer*

176. Going to open houses in Shaker, even if you are not looking for a house.
     —*Mark W., Shaker Heights*

177. Biking along the city streets ogling the big, grand houses—picking out my favorite—as soon as I win the lottery.
     —*Anne Gordon, Editor, Sunday, The Plain Dealer*

178. A wonderful climate for growing roses.
    —*Cathryn Kapp, President & Creative Director,
    Kapp & Associates*

179. It's the best place in the world to launch a
    career.
    —*Greg Harbaugh, NASA Space Shuttle Astronaut*

180. Only $7 to park at Jacobs Field. At Fenway Park, Boston, it's $15. In Chicago, they steal your car. In New York, they kill you and take your car.

    —*Dan Coughlin, Sportscaster, WJW TV-8*

181. Pierogies, kielbasi, Johnny's Bar.

    —*Les Roberts, Author*

182. There's a lot of voluntary work. There's broad leadership. If you want to get involved in something, you can, and a lot of people do.

   — *Thomas Bier, Director of Housing Research Program, Cleveland State University*

183. The best walk-in-and-browse library in the country.

    —*Steve W., Cleveland Heights*

184. The Soldiers and Sailors Monument on Public Square. Our town's national treasure for pigeon bombardment.

    —*Marc Wyse, President, Wyse Advertising*

185. Public golf. In the 90-or-so days of summer,
      you can play 18 holes of golf on a different
      public course every day. And every course
      within an hour's drive of the Soldiers and
      Sailors Monument on Public Square. This
      is true. Hard to believe, sure, but true.

      —*Harry B., Cleveland*

186

A St. Patrick's Day parade worth
skipping work for.

187. There's a good knit as far as the fabric of people who live here; it's a close-knit, hard-working community.

— *Brad Daugherty, Center, Cleveland Cavaliers*

188. Every Christmas my family goes to see the lights on Public Square, and there's always something new to see.

— *Christina A., Lakewood*

189. I like my Coventry neighborhood—it's one of the most pleasant and diverse areas, and the people are artists or people who like the arts and are very tolerant. People come here from out of town and are knocked out by it. (They're also astounded by the large homes and lush neighborhoods.)

    —*Harvey Pekar, Cartoonist, Creator of American Splendor Comics*

190. The ethnic and racial diversity of the community is, for the most part and on all levels, a reality which is celebrated and enjoyed.

—*Rev. Kenneth Chalker, 1st United Methodist Church, Cleveland*

191. I wouldn't trade our weather from May to October for anywhere in the U.S. We actually get a little bit more sun than the Sun Belt—New Orleans, Phoenix, Honolulu—but the rest of the year is the tradeoff.

    —*Dick Goddard, Meterologist, WJW TV-8*

192. I get plenty of opportunities to use my favorite snow shovel.

    —*Cindy D., North Olmsted*

193. Spirit. The go-go-go spirit led by the young Mayor White during his second term. Nothing seems to be impossible for this city to accomplish at this time.

    —*Sam Miller, Chairman of the Board & Treasurer, Forest City Enterprises*

194. The Big Egg, the coolest all-night spot in town.

    —*Magnolia N., Cleveland*

195. Lake View Cemetery: quite a gathering. Dead industrialists and inventors, even a U.S. President. All this combined with exceptional monuments in a nature sanctuary. I personally enjoy having a quiet picnic on John D. Rockefeller's plot.

—*Dale G., Lakewood*

196. High school hockey at Winterhurst Skating
      Rink.
      —*Pat J., Brooklyn*

197. Pancakes and sausage smothered in Ohio's
      best syrup at Burton's Maple Festival.
      —*Ellen A., Orange*

198. Just a good, basic rock-and-roll town. We don't have the artists like Detroit had Motown, but we were a breakout town for many famous acts, Bowie, Springsteen, and our enthusiasm brought the Rock and Roll Hall of Fame here.

—*Jane Scott, World's Oldest Rock Reporter, The Plain Dealer*

199. Riding my bike in the Cuyahoga Valley National Park and the Metroparks system. Where else in the country have we spent so much on hike and bike trails—for so few fair days?

  —*R. Douglas Cowan, President & CEO,*
  The Davey Tree Expert Company

The working Flats: still a a symbol of the industrial might that helped build a nation.

201. Going from needing a hot beverage to jump-start your body in the winter to needing an ice cold beverage in the summer to cool down.

 —*Perry Ganchar, Right Wing,*
 Cleveland Lumberjacks

202. The warmth and friendliness of the people always makes me glad I chose to stay here.

 —*Wilma Smith, Anchor, WJW TV-8*

203. The juicy season—going to Schaaf Rd. greenhouses for the first hothouse tomatoes of the spring.

   —*Mary Strassmeyer, The Plain Dealer*

204. Real estate prices that bring a smile to an Easterner's face.

   —*Dr. Richard Ehrlich, Executive Director, Western Reserve Historical Society*

205. Cleveland is a sports-loving city with loyal fans in all types of sports.
   —*Carlos Baerga, Second Basemen, Cleveland Indians*

206. Who needs space travel, when the best stadium mustard in the universe is right here?
   —*Bob M., Bay Village*

207. Water: In 38 years of living here, no one has ever said the water bill was too high, and the water tastes great.

    —*Joseph Roman, Executive Director, Cleveland Tomorrow*

208. Amish country, Geauga County—wonderful handcrafts and homemade furniture.

    —*Ned Whelan, Whelan Communications*

209. An outdoor concert at Nautica stage on a warm summer evening.
   —*Lorna Barrett, Anchor, WEWS TV-5*

210. Cleveland Freenet, the first community-access computer network and the local onramp to the Internet.
   —*Donald K., South Euclid*

211. When I visited Cleveland as a kid from a rural small town, the lights of Shaker Square dazzled me. Little did I know I'd later live there, 75 miles down the old Nickle Plate tracks, where I could be dazzled every day.

—*Richard Gildenmeister, bookseller*

212. No orange barrels for two months per year (Jan. & Feb.).

   —*Gib Shanley, Sportscaster, WUAB TV-43*

213. The park system: A great place to cross-country ski.

   —*Mary B., Hudson*

214. Commitment to the well-being of this community.

   —*Clayton Deutsch, Managing Director, McKinsey & Company*

215. A 15-minute commute to downtown. And three bucks to park all day. Considered fiction in Boston and NYC.

   —*David G., Cleveland Heights*

216. Can any city in America top Cleveland for producing such genuine, home grown television legends as Dorothy Fuldheim, Uncle Jake, Linn "Barnaby" Sheldon, Tom Field, Warren Guthrie, Dick Goddard, Alice Weston, Jim Graner, and Nev Chandler?
    —*Tim Taylor, Anchor, WJW TV-8*

217. Feagler's smile.
    —*Bill Gunlocke, Publisher*

218. The four seasons, the way they were meant to be: warm summers, a crisp fall, unpredictable winters, and a spring that starts it all over again.

    —*Steve W., Cleveland Heights*

219. Cheap air flights make it easy to get out of here in almost any direction.

    —*Morgan Lund, Actor*

220. What other city gives you a longer weather forecast than sports report on the late-night news?

—*Liz Ludlow, Editor, Cleveland Magazine*

221. Action-packed martial arts movies at the Cinematheque.

—*Jim N., Lyndhurst*

222

Paddling—or just drifting—along the Cuyahoga, Chagrin, or Rocky, Black, and Grand rivers.

223. Is there any other comparable metro area in the country with the plethora of high quality arts organizations? The list is endless: Ohio Chamber Orchestra, Cleveland Institute of Music, Cleveland Institute of Art, Cleveland Ballet and Opera, Apollo's Fire, Great Lakes Theater Festival, The Cleveland Play House, the Cleveland Chamber Music Society, Court and Countryside, the Art Museum Music Series, Chagrin Valley Playhouse, the Beck Center . . . well, you get the idea.

—*Robert Conrad, President and Broadcast Manager, WCLV FM-95.5*

224. The Great Lakes Brewing Company: Every great city needs its own beer; this is ours.
— *Michael Heaton, Minister of Culture, The Plain Dealer*

225. Chagrin River Road.
— *Jonathan Forman, Cedar Lee Theatre*

226. Blues: Robert Lockwood Jr., Aces & Eights,
   Mr. Stress Blues Band.

   —*Tom H., Cleveland*

227. The belief that anything below Interstate
   480 is in the south.

   —*Dr. Jerry Sue Thornton, President, Cuyahoga
   Community College, Metro Campus*

228. Discount stores galore. You can shop 'til you drop and never pay full price for anything!

   —*Denise J., Cleveland*

229. Home to the world's greatest football fans! Willing to sit in sub-zero weather, wear orange and brown, and never, never give up hope!

   —*Katherine Boyd, Reporter, WEWS TV-5*

230. The largest Chamber of Commerce in the country, the first with an African-American female as President.

    —*Paula F., Cleveland*

231. The world's best benefits for the world's best causes—from Mud Volleyball to the Animal Protective League.

    —*Rena Blumberg, Public Relations Director,*
    WDOK/WRMR

232. A sunny October day sailing on Lake Erie: winds out of the southwest at about 10 knots, temperature 68 degrees, glorious fall colors along the shoreline, my gorgeous husband at the helm, and two steamy mugs of mulled cider. HEAVEN!

   —*Lee Jordan, Anchor, Live on Five, WEWS TV-5*

233. Otto Graham, Larry Doby, Jim Brown—I grew up with the Walter Mitty dream of being the best in sports. I learned to love the Indians and hate the Yankees and that there's nothing wrong with being No. 2 in size as long as you believe you are No. 1 in quality.

—*Jack Kahl, Jr., Chairman and CEO, Manco, Inc.*

234. Variety is the spice of life, and Cleveland is variety.

   —*Mike and Sharon Hargrove, Manager and Manager-at-Large, Cleveland Indians*

235. Cleveland people are hospitable and make warm friends.

   —*Fred Crawford, Director Emeritus, TRW*

236.

(Add your own favorite Best Thing here.)

Have <u>Your</u> Say!
Official **Best Things in Life** *Response Card*

Here's my favorite *Best Thing* about Cleveland:

Name: _____

City of Residence: _____

Mail to: Gray & Co., Publishers • 11000 Cedar Avenue, Cleveland, Ohio 44106